When you purchase this book,

$5.00 will be donated to

the Hospice Care Center in Akron, Ohio.

GOD a LOGS
On
LIVING and DYING

By Sam Oliver

ISBN: 978-1-60414-048-4 / 1-60414-048-8

Other Books by Sam Oliver:

A Fish Named Ed

What the Dying Teach Us: Lessons on Living

*Integrating the Feminine Spirit:
Returning to the Womb of Creation*

Rhyme Runs Deep

A Life in Review

Blessings!

Sam Oliver

I DEDICATE THIS BOOK

"TO GOD"

Instructions on Using this Book

Have you ever wondered what a conversation with God would be like? In this book, I want you to imagine yourself talking to God and writing down the results. Do not think hard about what you want to say - just say it. You might be surprised what insights are inside you. If you want to talk about *anger* that day and notice it — do it. There is no right or wrong in how you write your own dialogue with God. It is your book to keep or refer back to at another time.

When I wrote these daily moments with God, I felt myself paying more attention to whatever it was that I was focusing on that day. For me, the insights took me to a place where judgments cease and the desire to understand became more prevalent. Such a view of living makes a person begin to seek first to understand, instead of, act on what a person understands to be life's point of view in any given moment. Life is much deeper than it appears on the surface. As we integrate this method of understanding life, we may find ourselves meeting each other in soul more often than personality. Although a persona is necessary for living, our personality does not have the capacity to move us into areas where life reveals itself to us from the depths of eternity itself.

This book is to help those who are caring for their dying loved ones record thoughts about living with dying. It is a book written directly to God or your Creator in a relationship manner. Each day, I would ask two questions: What do you want me to notice today? And, how can I get there? The words that followed were a direct inner hearing of what I believe God would say back to me. On the page that follows, I ask you to do the same. The first part of the question is to tune in on what I need to notice that day. The second question has two parts. I would concentrate on what

I need to do to create and experience the first question. Then, I would apply this to the dying process. The key to pulling this off on a deeper level than your beliefs about God is to imagine that YOU ARE talking to God, and that, GOD IS talking to you.

One final note, I want you to notice the words in italics. To me, these words were clear directives by God. These guiding forces/words of God were to be pondered. They were clearly my direction for the day and God's voice. On occasions, the day would be filled with people talking about what God wanted me to ponder for the day. In the section I ask you to imagine God speaking to you, there were times in this book that I spoke in the first person. At other times, I spoke in the second person. The reason for this is there were times that I just felt distant and times I felt closely directed by God's voice. It is the same in life and in death. It is my prayer as you do this journal that God's voice becomes clearer to you.

DAY 1

What do you want me to notice today?

First of all, I want you to move from a *"belief" to a "knowing"* in me. This shift in your awareness will allow you to have total faith and total trust in my care for you and the evolution of humanity. Society is used to trusting in their own wisdom; instead of, the wisdom that has created the moon, the stars, and the human heart.

How can I get there?

You will need to shift from self-centered awareness to life-centered awareness. The ego has the tendency to believe in what the ego knows to be real. I am asking you to trust me with your whole heart and soul, as though, your life depends on it. And, it does. You see, I am asking you to see through your eyes what you cannot see with them. For example, take a pebble and throw it into a pond. On the surface, you will see a ripple effect. You will see the effect of an action you took upon yourself to create.

As the pebble sinks deeper and deeper into the pond, there will come a time when you will no longer be able to see it anymore. Yet, you know that the pebble traveled to the bottom of the pond. How did it get there? Here is where you begin to see through your eyes what you cannot see with them. If you paid close attention to this experience, you will notice that your imagination and your heart were engaged. This allowed you to see from within what you could not see externally and "know" it was a real experience without having a personal experience of what was happening before you.

Dying people are on a similar journey. They have to trust that an inner path is being created for them in their soul. They know that one day they will close their eyes to the world around them and open them up in a place created by the wisdom that brought them into this world. In many ways, dying people show us the way into eternity through their dying. The closer a dying person gets to death — the more introspective they and their loved ones become. At the moment of death, loved ones who are left behind begin to shift their attention from a relationship based on the personality to one where souls meet.

YOUR TURN

What do you want me to notice today?

_____

_____

_____

_____

_____

How can I get there?

_____

_____

_____

_____

_____

_____

_____

_____

_____

Dying people remind us that…
_____

_____

_____

_____

_____

_____

_____

_____

_____

_____

_____

_____

_____

_____

_____

_____

_____

_____

_____

_____

DAY 2

What do you want me to notice today?

Today, I want you to share *grace*. It is interesting that people seem to think this is something one receives each day. It is often something experienced after one has done something wrong or not done something one could have done in a particular situation. And somehow, life has a way of smoothing things out. Over time, we find that past experiences whereby something caused harm or a change of direction in our lives gave us meaning, hope, and healing at a later point in our lives.

Most people live their lives as though they expect life to always go their way. If you look back upon your life, you know this is not the case. Grace is knowing life will have it's ups and it's downs and knowing it is all worth the journey.

How can I get there?

Try this. No matter what comes your way today — face it with the understanding that you are not alone and you have what it takes to make it through whatever comes your way. This kind of confidence comes through you and not from you. We all receive from life far more than we give to it. You will find that it is true. How does the world survive with such patterns of behavior from our Creator? If you were to simply ponder this one notion itself, you will be in amazement all day long.

Consider this, from the moment you are born until you are 18, there is no way you can ever repay your parents for all they have done for you. There is no way. It doesn't end here though. Life is simply this way. Think about it and be grateful.

All the silly little mistakes we make each day in our jobs, our family, and our friends. We would not be able to obtain any level of intimacy without grace. Today, give thanks to your Creator for such a magical place, created in a way, to make us all destined for unconditional love.

In my work as a Hospice Chaplain, I witness dying people realize just how fortunate they were in having been given so much. This is not to say that sadness and anger are not present. If you look a little closer, sadness and anger are the result of being grateful for what we have been given and not wanting to let it go.

YOUR TURN

What do you want me to notice today?

_____

_____

_____

_____

_____

How can I get there?

_____

_____

_____

_____

_____

_____

_____

_____

Dying people remind us that…

_____

_____

_____

_____

_____

_____

_____

_____

_____

_____

_____

_____

_____

_____

_____

_____

DAY 3

What do you want me to notice today?

Forgive everyone, everyday, and in every way. Each person is doing the best he or she can. No one, absolutely no one is perfect. Since no one is perfect, this means that we all need to share more patience and more understanding surrounding all aspects of our interactions with one another. Think of the last time you needed to forgive someone. And, think of the last time you needed to be forgiven. When we need to be forgiven, there is a feeling of lack or something is missing. When we need to forgive, we often feel anger. Anger is a secondary emotion for loss. When we lose something, the need to restore what was lost. This sends us on a search within ourselves for attention in a peace filled direction. If you noticed, to forgive or to be forgiven leads you to the same place. Both paths of awareness lead us on a search. What are you searching for? You are searching to find wholeness. What is wholeness? This is often one's perception of reality created by what one believes to be true. This creation of what one believes to be true is the path of one's soul seeking manifestation in the world of form from the formless.

How can I get there?

There is no set way to wholeness. Simply being aware that you have a self-defined understanding of wholeness that is within you is what we simply need to give attention to within us. This continued attention on what we seek the most within us will grow in our awareness until the need to place our attention on forgiveness fades away.

If a person was to believe that forgiveness is something obtained through the human psyche alone, we all would find the journey into such a place within us as something to avoid. In the deepest parts of who we are, we want to connect to what is sacred within us. Therefore, to re-create a past interaction with someone who we feel we harmed or who we feel harmed us is a useless attempt to embrace what cannot be. This is not to say that certain relationships close to us do not need verbal efforts to make up for a past action leading to harm. In fact, a person can find this useful, and even, helpful. The point I want to make is the place one's attention may be at the time such a verbal interaction will become vital in the success of such expressions taking place.

Dying patients remind me that there are countless times in all our lives where the issue of forgiveness was perceived and we become aware of it. There is no way a dying person can retrieve all their past life experiences in physical form, but we can recall these moments in time and visualize how we would have handled them differently. This is our soul seeking to make right a wrong our personality may not allow us to do, or it may no longer be feasible to take place in our current circumstances. People are such a vast array of experiences. There are endless paths of attention within us calling for our attention. Perhaps, the instant we remember who we are and who others are in the deepest parts of our being, we begin to remember the love that brings all our lives together, and into, being. This remembrance of who we are as children of our Creator reminds us of the unconditional spirit reflected within our own selves. The transcendence of flesh and blood inspires us to give our Creator our lives, the lives of others, and our very reason for living into the hands that created us.

YOUR TURN

What do you want me to notice today?

_____

_____

_____

_____

_____

How can I get there?

_____

_____

_____

_____

_____

_____

_____

_____

Dying people remind us that…

DAY 4

What do you want me to notice today?

I want you to *care about other people* today. When you focus on caring for others, something profound happens to you. Your attention will shift. You will move from self-centered awareness to life-centered awareness. Believe me, life centered awareness is a much greater perspective. Here, you will find yourself making decisions based on what is needed as a whole; rather than, needs based on fulfilling your own personal objectives.

How can I get there?

When you begin to realize that you are part of a much greater awareness, some of your personal challenges seem smaller. Why? You will notice that everyone has needs, wants, and desires. Many times in life, we focus way too much on ourselves and not the needs of others. If you do this too much, you will become isolated and let no one into your life. Although there are times when you do need alone time to charge your batteries from so much outward focus, you will find that fully focusing on what you are doing for others is a distraction from self-centered awareness.

At the end of the day, do take some time for yourself. You will need to find ways to balance the needs of others with the needs of the self. In the end, you will notice that one of the greatest gifts we do have to give to others is to give our lives away knowing we have helped another person's day become a little bit better. This will also meet your own need to fulfill your reason for living or purpose in life.

Not long ago, I did a funeral for a man whose wife asked him to share with her the most important thing in life he could think of at the time. Without hesitation, he told her that the most important thing in life is to "care about other people." He was a man who had won several awards for the contributions he made in the community. He was a Psychology Professor and planted many many seeds in the souls of his students. These seeds of awareness will allow his students to have perspective and have a purpose filled life for years to come. In caring about other's needs, this Professor will live on from generation to generation to generation.

YOUR TURN

What do you want me to notice today?

_____

_____

_____

_____

_____

How can I get there?

_____

_____

_____

_____

_____

_____

_____

_____

Dying people remind us that…

DAY 5

What do you want me to notice today?

In all ways and in all living things, I want you to see the *abundance* that is all around you. You are surrounded by energy and information from people and sources of love such as animals and sacred places that give you peace. Enjoy it. Use it. There is not a single stone left unturned. All was thought of and given to you the moment you were born. There is nothing you can't achieve. What you desire - desires you. Desires don't just show up in you without me finding ways to help you with those desires. Focus on the needs of your soul. What is calling for your attention? All is supplied on earth and in heaven to help you create that which you keep firmly in your vision.

How can I get there?

This is the easy part. Just keep your vision in your heart, mind, and soul. Like I said before, abundance is all around you. You will be given clues to help support the longings of your soul to be made known and revealed for the purposes of increasing your faith in me and the place I have directed you in life and in living. Never forget that you are a soul with infinite possibilities waiting to be born. You will need to focus and keep this inner vision constantly before you. I will bring people with the gifts and talents you need to fulfill the mission you feel your calling in life is directing you into every moment and every day. There is no limit to what I want to give to you. All I ask in return is that you trust. You need to trust in me as though your life, your soul, and your calling depends on it.

If you were a dying patient, you would have to trust me as though your life depended on it. This kind of trust is what I want from you. This kind of trust will give you peace in knowing that all can and should be yours through such a strong connection to the wisdom that brought you into this world, and somehow, knows how to lead you home. It is not as important to know where you are going, as much as, it is to know whom you're following. I WILL LEAD YOU TO ABUNDANCE. By the way, you are sitting right in the middle of it.

YOUR TURN

What do you want me to notice today?

_____

_____

_____

_____

_____

How can I get there?

_____

_____

_____

_____

_____

_____

_____

_____

Dying people remind us that…

DAY 6

What do you want me to notice today?

On this day, I want you to listen to my *still small voice*. Do you remember when you were a child and didn't pay attention to your parents, and heard, "you have your own mind?" Everyone has this tendency to listen to the voice of their desires and intentions. What I want you to pay particular attention to is where the voices inside you lead you. They are voices of fear and love. Follow the voice that leads you to peace and to love. I will be waiting for you there.

How can I get there?

Throughout a person's lifetime, there are various voices calling for his or her attention. Because experience informs us, we learn which voice to follow that leads us to chaos or to peace. This voice does not get louder over time. The voice of spirit becomes clearer to us through experience. We learn to follow paths of existence that have the tendency to guide us to a feeling of being at home. Over time, we build relationships with people and things that determine our soul's path and reveal our soul's desire to be made known. Our moment to moment decisions to follow the presence of what is most sacred to us manifests itself.

Dying people listen and find themselves moving from listening to the words outside themselves to listening to the words inside themselves. These inner connections to words of direction enables a dying loved one to withdraw from the world around them and integrate their souls to those who have gone before them. These eternal connections have a voice that always has and always will call us to our most authentic self.

YOUR TURN

What do you want me to notice today?

_____

_____

_____

_____

_____

How can I get there?

_____

_____

_____

_____

_____

_____

_____

_____

Dying people remind us that…

DAY 7

What do you want me to notice today?

I want you to *seek me*. When you find me, you will know my direction for you. So many times in life, people forget to seek me for direction. The lack of energy and the lack of focus is the end result. Look for me, you will find me when you begin to see through your heart what you cannot see with your eyes.

How can I get there?

While looking through your eyes at someone or something, try to place your attention on what is going on inside you. The moment you simultaneously look outside yourself while looking within yourself through the inner vision of your mind or material realities, you will find that a connectedness is taking place. You will feel whole. What your emotions or your thoughts are on doesn't matter as much as simply just being in that moment. Judgments are not necessary and keep you from being in the moment of reflection needed to find me. Unconditional love is all around you and in you. Just perceive life as sacred with the potential for eternal love and you will find my Spirit creating and deepening who you really are.

"The things in life that really matter are the things in life that isn't matter." I have been saying this for years and not sure where it comes from. Yet, this statement as well as all statements worth listening to came through someone; rather than, from someone. This is the free flowing nature of life and the place of attention a dying patient is led into as he or she is awakening into their most authentic self — their soul.

YOUR TURN

What do you want me to notice today?

_____

_____

_____

_____

How can I get there?

_____

_____

_____

_____

_____

_____

_____

_____

Dying people remind us that…

DAY 8

What do you want me to notice today?

There are many distractions in the world. This would be a good day for you to *focus*. Focus on your needs, as well as, the needs of others. Keep the needs of yourself and the needs of others in balance. You will notice that you and others have this need to keep life in balance. There is a delicate balance in nature to give and receive. Take an apple tree. An apple tree begins to grow. It will then mature. If you pick the apples too soon, they will taste sour. If you pick the apples too late another taste of sour springs forth as a rotten taste. In the middle of these two extremes is the sweetness of an apple's maturity. The apple's time has come to give back before it dies. And oh, how good the ripe tasting texture of an apple whose time has come to give in due season.

How can I get there?

You have been in training since the moment you were born. You have been learning and growing from various experiences that teach you and develop you into becoming a mature adult. Along the way, your elders have been sharing with you their wisdom and their love and care. When you mature into adulthood, it is time for you to share with those around you gifts you have learned since being a child. Just like the apple, you are ripe and ready to share with the public those seeds of awareness given to you since birth. You are ready for the community and the world to literally use or taste the talents you have to give.

Dying people have physical bodies that no longer serve them or the community in a way that they did in their prime. Like the apple, everything dies in due season. At the same time, a dying person's worth to society is probably more valuable to those who care for them. Dying people are becoming more soul than body. They are transforming right before our eyes. Their attention turns inward and the virtues and values they have lived through in their lifetime become more vivid than any other phase of their life. They teach us what is important and share their stories with us from their heart and soul. Stories create images in our mind and elicit emotions from the feelings expressed by the storyteller.

It can be as though you were there as you feel and see inwardly what a dying person shares with you. Memories expressed in tranquility come from the soul. They fill all of us with a knowing that who we are now is a result of our past expressions on material reality. Dying people teach us to live in soul long before we die and plant seeds of eternity inside. When it is our time to close our eyes to the world around us and open them up to a place where eternity itself dwells. We will have arrived where we started in life and call it home.

YOUR TURN

What do you want me to notice today?

_____

_____

_____

_____

_____

How can I get there?

_____

_____

_____

_____

_____

_____

_____

_____

Dying people remind us that…

DAY 9

What do you want me to notice today?

Concentrate on *effort*. All of life is energy and information. Seeds of awareness are in constant growth. "Where one's attention goes - energy flows." I am sure you have heard this many times. It is true. Life comes through you and not from you. Life is the greatest gift a person can receive upon this earth.

How can I get there?

One way you can notice if life is moving through you; instead of, life as moving from you is to pay attention. When life is coming from you, you are using a lot of personal effort to achieve a task. When life is moving through you, you are embracing and acknowledging the need for and dependence on your Creator's strength to sustain you each day and each moment of your life.

Let's just say you are on earth to fulfill a mission, a purpose, or a reason for being. As you act out this intention and desire to fill your reason for being on earth, your mind is clear and

51

your body is filled with joy, energy, and contentment. As you get feedback from others who are the recipients of your purpose on earth, what returns to you is the gratitude for being the person this experience is transferred through. Your highest joy is not the praise or the servant being willing to serve another. The real joy is in knowing you were chosen for the spirit of one's Creator to flow through you and create in you a clean heart where purity exists. It is our way of knowing ourselves as God knows us. It is a deep connection with God in that moment. This level of effort is simply your faith, your trust, your willingness to integrate yourself into the fabric of God's spirit moving through your being. This level of connectedness is the effortless effort of being present as you become a vessel for God's hands, feet, mind, and body to work through in accomplishing God's will for your life and the lives of others.

Hospice patients clearly understand effort and the need to let God, those God works through, or one's Higher Power bring to them their sustenance each day. When you were a child, life was effortless. You needed someone to take care of your needs, so you could live and grow into independence. When we die, we need help as well. We need help in letting go of personal effort and allowing God to fill us with faith. When we let go of personal effort, God/Our Creator can fill us up with spirit and the realization that we do nothing alone. Then, the resources that are available to us move to our aid and help us with our transition from being born into this world, and to, the birth that takes us into eternity.

YOUR TURN

What do you want me to notice today?

_____

_____

_____

_____

_____

How can I get there?

_____

_____

_____

_____

_____

_____

_____

_____

Dying people remind us that…

_____
_____
_____
_____
_____
_____
_____
_____
_____
_____
_____
_____
_____
_____
_____
_____
_____
_____
_____
_____

DAY 10

What do you want me to notice today?

I want you to be *proactive* today. There are people in this world who are reactive and those who are proactive. To be proactive is a "choice" I want you to make today. Each day we have choices to make on how we see the world around us. The choice for a proactive lifestyle enables you to know your authentic self. Your authentic self is empowering no matter what your life circumstances.

How can I get there?

Inside us all is the capacity to do good. It is a choice toward your most authentic self. As we listen to and embrace with our soul our most authentic self, we feel strength and energy moving in and through us. When we do not listen to and embrace our most authentic self, we feel drained.

Dying patients in Hospice Care remind us who we really are. They share with us stories and insights into the nature of soul.

They use their imagination and their heart to reveal experiences of their past by pulling this energy and information into the present. A dying loved one does not act in the world in the same way as he or she did while younger and with more vitality. When we lose this part of us or the personality, we retreat inside ourselves by closing our eyes to the world around us and opening them up to the inner path being created before us. We can fight this journey, or we can make a "choice" to live in the path opening up to us in our dying. In essence, dying people are dying into life.

YOUR TURN

What do you want me to notice today?

_____

_____

_____

_____

_____

How can I get there?

_____

_____

_____

_____

_____

_____

_____

_____

Dying people remind us that…

DAY 11

What do you want me to notice today?

Are you *balanced*? What is balance for you? People often use external measures to tell if they are balanced or not. Life is often determined by what we do and what we do not do. How do we really know any measures of balance are correct? Are there any? The answers to these questions of balance lie in the questions themselves. If you have to use external measures to determine one's state of well being, you may already need some help in remembering who you are.

How can I get there?

For centuries, our ancestors didn't use measuring cups to determine how full or not full they were at the end of a meal. They worked until they were tired. And, they slept until they woke up. These days, people even have to go so far as to schedule personal time with one another. Much of our daily experiences are determined by outside resources and external circumstances.

What do you think would happen if we were to follow our instincts? Many of us would not know what direction in life to go. We are so used to following external signs. Inside us, there is an internal mechanism, a guiding force, our creativity waiting to be made known in our lives. Perhaps, this is our bliss. It may be our purpose to fulfill in life. It may even be our destiny.

For over 18 years, I have been working with actively dying people who are in an unconscious state. Dying folks are not so concerned about where they are going, as much as, "whom" they are following. Have you ever set at the bedside of a loved one and watched them look, as if, in space? You may have seen and heard a dying loved one talk to loved ones who have already passed on into Eternity. It doesn't, seemingly, make sense to embrace one's dying. The ego cannot and will not for fear of its own existence coming to a close. Maybe the key to finding balance lies "in" remembering who we are. Here, our focus is on life and not on the self. This allows us to focus our attention on what flows through us. You and I at this point are no longer focused on our personal energy "where our energy begins and ends." Instead, our focus is on being in life, and not, separate from life as though life depends on our existence. When there is no beginning and no ending to life and self awareness, you are one continuous flow of energy. Life then becomes a seamless thread whereby one part of life stacks on top of another with no interruptions or pauses. This may be our greatest existence in the state of balance. And, when we are free from the body's awareness, we are free in soul awareness and free to be in "whole" awareness.

YOUR TURN

What do you want me to notice today?

_____

_____

_____

_____

_____

How can I get there?

_____

_____

_____

_____

_____

_____

_____

_____

_____

Dying people remind us that…

DAY 12

What do you want me to notice today?

I want you to *reflect on the funeral service* you officiated this morning. Did you notice how many people were present and all the tears that surfaced? What did you notice in the room as more and more people arrived? Did it feel different? In what ways did this room feel different?

How can I get there?

As the room began to fill with loved ones in grief, the room began to feel full. There was a warm feeling in a room that once felt cold when the room was empty. It is as though the memories are a living presence inside us. A relationship that was once outside us, is now, completely inside us. This movement into an eternal relationship with our deceased loved one enables us to experience how deep our relationships really are, and how, relationships move our attention into the heart.

Dying people deepen something inside us. They move our awareness into a place where souls meet and encounter one another in places that cannot be measured in depth or height. This limitless capacity to form relationships in one's soul acts as a path. It is a direction for our soul to enter into who we really are. This pathless path into our soul allows us to get a taste of our destiny. It is the destiny of us all to return to where we came from at birth. Such wisdom knows the way home. Such wisdom creates us in a way that we long for and find meaning in what does not always make sense. It is the longing of our soul to return to what created us.

YOUR TURN

What do you want me to notice today?

_____

_____

_____

_____

_____

How can I get there?

_____

_____

_____

_____

_____

_____

_____

_____

Dying people remind us that…

DAY 13

What do you want me to notice today?

I want you to *overcome challenges*. Challenges are all around us. They create something inside you nothing else can. Challenges bring out qualities of attention that make you a person you were not before these things happen. You are transformed.

How can I get there?

Trans Form basically means to go beyond form. Transformation takes place when we focus our attention in an area of living we are not used to living in. Our experience of insight/to see from within enables us to draw into our heart and soul new energy and new information. As we work with and put into practice these sudden notions upon a new territory and a new reality for ourselves — we change. We become different people the moment we trust a path in front of us we have never walked before.

Dying people have a tremendous challenge in front of them. They are to trust in what they cannot see. A dying person is to trust

Sam Oliver

with complete abandonment the path into the unknown. This has the tendency to move all people around them into introspective awareness. It is a movement into faith and trust in a power greater than themselves. Such is the case with challenges. Challenges are opportunities to move our attention away from the problems of living and find hidden pathways inside us that can stir us into new directions. These new directions may become directives and guides for living in ways that can lead us into brighter and better ways of experiencing our lives.

YOUR TURN

What do you want me to notice today?

_____

_____

_____

_____

_____

How can I get there?

_____

_____

_____

_____

_____

_____

_____

_____

Dying people remind us that…

DAY 14

What do you want me to notice today?

I want you to reflect on *things of the past*. Memories are lived experiences pondered in the heart and the imagination. The problem most people have with their memories are the reliving of their memories over and over again as though the past is real in the present. This can be a good thing if our memories are used to build our self-esteem and our self-worth.

How can I get there?

Notice how you feel when you wake up in the morning. Doesn't it feel as though you are awakening to a new day? If you were to live each day as though you have no past and no future, every moment you have on that day would be a gift. You would experience each second as though it were your last. The truth is that this is more true than we know. All any of us have is the present. When we bring past experiences into present encounters, there is no way we can experience what is in front of us with our full attention. When we bring future anticipations into our present moment, there is no way we can experience the present moment with our full attention as well.

Dying patients experience each moment as though it is their last one. Every day is sacred. It is an opportunity to take in their life as never before. There is something about knowing one's days are numbered that allows us to be purposeful in all we do and all we are. If you knew your days were numbered and close to the end, would you live this moment, this day, in a different way? I hope your answer is no, but I suspect most of us would have to say yes. Don't leave this world with memories of regrets. Leave this world knowing you lived fully until you died.

YOUR TURN

What do you want me to notice today?

_____

_____

_____

_____

_____

How can I get there?

_____

_____

_____

_____

_____

_____

_____

_____

Dying people remind us that…

_____

_____

_____

_____

_____

_____

_____

_____

_____

_____

_____

_____

_____

_____

_____

_____

_____

_____

_____

_____

_____

_____

_____

DAY 15

What do you want me to notice today?

I want you to *envision* your future. This is what dreams are made of over the course of a lifetime. A dream is an inner vision of how you want life to be. In these dreams, a person is filled with joy, imagination, and heart. A person literally enjoys imagining one's heart's desire. Then, to bring one's dream into reality, one has to trust by engaging in behaviors that are steps toward goals to achieve one's vision.

How can I get there?

To fulfill one's vision requires faith in what you cannot presently see. To see through your eyes what you cannot see with them requires faith, hope, and love. Bringing about one's vision requires only two things: a trust in your dream and a trust in your Creator to bring about the necessary people, information, and circumstances to enliven your dream with material reality.

A dying person readily does this in prayer. In prayer, a person closes their eyes to the world around them and opens their eyes into the world of spirit. Here, anything can happen you focus your attention upon. Where your attention goes, energy flows into that direction activating the imagination to create into form from the formless your ultimate desires and intentions. Heaven is just a moment away. Heaven is the fulfillment of where your attention takes you. It is the journey from here to there without taking a single step. The kingdom of heaven is indeed within you.

YOUR TURN

What do you want me to notice today?

_____

_____

_____

_____

_____

How can I get there?

_____

_____

_____

_____

_____

_____

_____

_____

_____

Dying people remind us that…

DAY 16

What do you want me to notice today?

This is the day I want you to *know the power of choice*. I want you to know you always have the power of choice. In any situation, you have the power to choose how you are going to enter into it. Even when experiences seem a certain way, this is an illusion. Think of any situation you have encountered in life. There are always options. It is US that chooses whether to or not to view life from a narrow or much broader view.

How can I get there?

When you have a problem to solve, there is a goal you would like to reach. Usually, the end goal has something to do with the problem solved. How we get there is another story. When a writer begins to form a story, he or she does not know how he or she will get to the end. Even if a writer has an assumption on how the story will end, something in the formation of their story begins to come alive. It is often a good thing that the story of our lives does not turn out the way we had hoped for none of us have that much knowledge.

If we did have all knowledge on living just described, we would be so busy helping ourselves and others try to understand what we possess. I believe this is God's job. At the same time, we would not be able to know ourselves as we truly are. And then, we would know so much that the need for Our Creator would not exist, and would, we?

It may seem that dying people do not have a choice. Well, dying people do, in fact, have a choice. They have the power to review what has led them to the point of death. They have the experience of their lives to fall back on. Through reflecting on living, the good and the bad choices lived, one can see in these choices a tremendous power. The power of a living Creator that has given us much more in life than we have or will ever give back to it. You see, beyond the body fading and becoming more soul than body, there is a spirit of awareness that realizes all we have experienced and will ever experience is the wisdom that has created all we have known, know, and will ever know in the future.

Even in death itself, I hope you can see that we have the power to choose life. Life is the openness to experience each moment as it is and let it unfold through you whether in body or in soul.

YOUR TURN

What do you want me to notice today?

_____

_____

_____

_____

_____

How can I get there?

_____

_____

_____

_____

_____

_____

_____

_____

_____

Dying people remind us that…

_____

_____

_____

_____

_____

_____

_____

_____

_____

_____

_____

_____

_____

_____

_____

_____

_____

_____

_____

_____

DAY 17

What do you want me to notice today?

Pay attention to *where people place their attention.* When you speak to someone, you will hear the voice of fear and/or the voice of love. All awareness comes from someone's heart and their soul. The way a person views the world is digested inside them. What comes out of a person's mouth and actions are what is inside them. Take an apple for example. What kind of juice is squeezed out of an apple. The answer is apple juice. We can only share what is inside us.

How can I get there?

You and I can begin to discipline ourselves. Where our attention remains in constant awareness, there will be experiences of various sorts that will rise up into our lives. Take time to do a test. Smile at others, and then, notice that most people will smile back at you. On the other hand, try frowning at others and see how many will not smile back at you.

A dying person's attention turns inward over time especially at the end of life. Now, take a look where people's attention goes who love this dying person. Your loved ones tend to turn their attention inward and remember the good and the bad times they had with their loved one. Overall, most people remember the good and forgive the bad times. Inside us all, there is a deep desire to give and receive unconditional love. When our attention turns inward and into the heart, we can only give to others what is inside us. It is here we meet in the greatest aspect of attention known to humanity — love.

YOUR TURN

What do you want me to notice today?

_____

_____

_____

_____

How can I get there?

_____

_____

_____

_____

_____

_____

_____

_____

Dying people remind us that…

DAY 18

What do you want me to notice today?

Look for *the innocence in others.* Everyone is born into the world with it. We never lose it. Yet, the experiences of our lives tend to make us feel as though we have. Inside every person, there is a child that knows how to trust the world and the people in it.

How can I get there?

Here is the key that will open the door to innocence. <u>Believe in people</u>. Each of us has different gifts and talents that no one else has. We have different experiences along the way that have taught us a unique perspective on the world and how to use our talents in a way no one else has, is, or ever will. We are here for a purpose. We are here to fulfill experiences no one else can. To judge whether or not what we do is good or bad may lead to questioning God's purpose for people.

Have you ever noticed how dying people do not seem to have energy to be judgmental? I am talking about close to the end. They either do not have the energy for it or even care. When a person comes to end of living life in a body, there seems to be such an identification with purity and innocence born out of forgiveness for one's own self that extending this to others comes naturally. We learn to love, and we learn to hate. When we return to soul, we remember who we are. We return to unconditional love. We return to innocence.

YOUR TURN

What do you want me to notice today?

_____

_____

_____

_____

_____

How can I get there?

_____

_____

_____

_____

_____

_____

_____

_____

Dying people remind us that…

DAY 19

What do you want me to notice today?

I want you to *let go* today. Let go of control and your direction in life. Simply try to follow a presence of awareness known to you as peace, joy, and love. Let these guiding forces carry you from one experience to the next one. Let each moment fill you with your soul's purpose to find Me as your God seeking you.

How can I get there?

When we are born, we begin the process of developing our ego. Our personality seeks attention. This is the part of us we begin to identify as being real in this world. As we age, we begin to have such mastery in the world we tend to convince ourselves that what we see, touch, feel, taste, and hear are real. We convince ourselves that what is in the material reality is what gives us life.

Dying people spend a great deal of time seeking out what is real. Since he or she has to let go of the roles he or she has lived out in life, dying patients begin to sense a deep existence to their lives not defined by their senses. There is a spacial quality of existence to us just behind our persona or personality. This existence is our ability to be aware of our awareness. When we reach this quality of attention, we are free from the boundaries of space and time to define our existence. We become nothing, and in becoming nothing, we are free to embrace who we really are. Such a quality of existence can never die, and one's soul is embraced in eternity itself. Here, we find ourselves no longer a single entity, but rather, a part of the whole. We are a part of the universe itself, instead of, a separate and unique person within the whole. It is here a dying person calls home and rests in a level of awareness not made with human hands.

YOUR TURN

What do you want me to notice today?

_____

_____

_____

_____

_____

How can I get there?

_____

_____

_____

_____

_____

_____

_____

_____

Dying people remind us that…

DAY 20

What do you want me to notice today?

Did you know there is a difference between seeking and *guidance*? Seeking is looking for God's presence and direction. Guidance is a knowing through reflection and sometimes while we are in the midst of a situation whereby you know God's hand is upon you. Seeking is the effort you make to connect to God. Guidance is the realization that God has been with you all along and holding you in God's attention and direction.

How can I get there?

First of all, you can always know that God's hand is on you. There are times when you look back in life and realize that God had to have intervened in circumstances beyond your control. You received favor when you did not deserve such grace. This is usually in situations when others have control over the path in your life you are seeking to place your life in at the time. When we reflect on these times in life, we can see where our Creator was looking after our greatest good. We probably would not have been happy unless things went as they did. If we look closer, we may find that the place our Creator led us to was our soul's capacity to find fulfillment.

Dying people rely on guidance. No one seeks death in a "healthy state of mind." The ego wants to live. In our dying, guidance requires people to look within themselves for a journey into what creates complete surrender. This takes guidance to find peace in such a journey. Only one's soul can be drawn to such a quality of existence. It is the place we call eternity. It is our destiny to return to who we really are.

YOUR TURN

What do you want me to notice today?

_____

_____

_____

_____

_____

How can I get there?

_____

_____

_____

_____

_____

_____

_____

_____

Dying people remind us that…

DAY 21

What do you want me to notice today?

Transformation happens every day and every moment. Pay attention to how insights and information changes people. It gives us direction. It may even give some a purpose in life. Thus, enabling some people to stay focused on a particular path in life. Trans Form means to go beyond form. To see through your eyes what you can't see with them. This ability to draw into our being what we want to see happen in life gives us the courage to face one life experience after another. Throughout our stages of development and the various body forms from infancy to death, we are constantly becoming a different form along life's pathway.

How can I get there?

Life comes through us, and not, from us. All that moves in and through the experiences of our lives first came from a notion of what life could be like through the inner vision of our mind called the imagination. When you experience the feelings surrounding this inner picture in your heart, the mind and body connect to what is known as the soul. The soul is the bridge between what is and what is yet to be. The infusion of spirit or the inspiration that fuels our transformation is infinite, limitless, and eternal. There are times in our lives that we are redirected on our path to our Creator. This movement from one experience to another is our creative imagination in process of creating form out of the formless. As we stay with this path, our destiny begins to emerge.

Dying people know this path into the unknown very well. It is the only path available to them after a certain point in one's realization that their physical body is going to cease. What remains is one's capacity to be aware of their awareness. This awareness of one's awareness is the place of consciousness that no longer needs a body or personality to define one's unique expression in the world. In this place where one is connected to all living beings without judgment, and in, unconditional love, is the place called eternal love. Thus, allowing our lives to come full circle. Here, we end our lives as we began it - in the very wisdom that has created us.

YOUR TURN

What do you want me to notice today?

_____

_____

_____

_____

_____

How can I get there?

_____

_____

_____

_____

_____

_____

_____

_____

Dying people remind us that…

DAY 22

What do you want me to notice today?

Do you feel *protected*? This is a safe feeling I want you to notice. It has the appearance of self-confidence, but it goes much deeper inside you. When you feel safe, you can be yourself. You can act in ways that expresses your most authentic self. There is not a fear of rejection. There is the feeling of being blessed, known, cared for, and wanted.

How can I get there?

I want you to look deep inside yourself to the day you rode your bike for the first time. You may have watched others do this and one day decided you wanted to do the same. You get on that bike and can't balance yourself. You try to peddle and fall. You get on this bike another time and tell yourself to peddle harder and find that you fall harder. You find yourself frustrated and fear getting hurt. Then, you reach down deep inside yourself and say that you no longer care if you get hurt. You are going to ride that bike just like everyone else. This shift from bodily awareness to your soul revealing life before you enables you to experience a higher awareness guiding you. And, just like magic, you start peddling that bike as though you have all your life. You feel free. Inside this kind of awareness is the feeling of being protected. It is a womb like state whereby one's deepest self knows they will be ok.

Dying people reach this level of awareness inside themselves at a certain point in their dying. They move from fearing pain and suffering to identifying with no longer fearing what happens to their body. They become focused on becoming more soul than body. This creates in a dying patient incredible faith in embracing who they really are - a protected child of God.

YOUR TURN

What do you want me to notice today?

_____

_____

_____

_____

_____

How can I get there?

_____

_____

_____

_____

_____

_____

_____

_____

Dying people remind us that…

DAY 23

What do you want me to notice today?

Trust requires so much of us. Notice how much we trust one another in our daily lives. When you need healthcare, doctors are there to help you. When need psychological help, a friend or counselor is there to listen. When you need a home, there are carpenters, real estate agents, mortgage loaners, etc...

How can I get there?

As you can see, trust is how we live in this world. There is no way around this thing called trust. When you were born into this world, you trusted your parents to care for you. This kind of trust is born in innocence. What about the times when our trust in someone or ourselves is broken? What do we do then? If you are like most of us, we go to God. There is wisdom in our willingness to trust our Creator.

There is another kind of trust. We call this kind of trust experience. After living in this world for a time, we have many experiences we learn from. These experiences mature us. This maturity is our lived experiences. We can share them with others who are less experienced or share them with a friend as a way of relating and being of comfort.

Dying people realize and utilize both experience and innocence in trusting the wisdom of our Creator. There comes a moment when someone is dying that their experiences have led them back to where they started into this world. The difference is that we move from trusting our parents to care for us to the One who created all living things. This kind of trust requires all of us, as though, our very lives depended on it. And, it does.

YOUR TURN

What do you want me to notice today?

_____

_____

_____

_____

_____

How can I get there?

_____

_____

_____

_____

_____

_____

_____

_____

Dying people remind us that…

DAY 24

What do you want me to notice today?

Disorientation is a challenge for those going through it. This comes to us when we have more than we can handle mentally and emotionally at one given time. It is our signal to slow down and let life reveal to you what are the most important things and people to pay attention to moment by moment. We tend to try to do everything at once. Sometimes, we need to realize what is most necessary will be revealed and all other important matters will make themselves known in due time.

How can I get there?

Take time to breathe and notice where your attention will go when lack of focus is present. Notice how your attention will move to your forehead, and how, you will become short of breath. Try to draw your attention to your forehead and combine it with your heart and breathe deeply. Allow yourself to clear your mind of all responsibilities until you get your wits about you. When your breath becomes deeper, begin to think about your day and your responsibilities.

Dying patients at Hospice go through this from time to time. They have a lot to deal with at one time. It is sometimes difficult to slow one's thinking down and settle one's emotions when you are faced with death. Take a look at death. What comes to a close is our physical body not able to act in the world in the same way as before. Also, what comes to a close is one's ego. Our self importance and acting in the world can always be replaced, but our uniqueness will never be replaced. Once a person realizes that he or she has fulfilled a purpose in life that no one else has, can, or ever will - he or she can accept that their role in life is done. Behind one's personality or role(s) in life is what infuses our lives into being, and the one whose body is coming to an end can find peace in what lies beyond itself. It is here people become integrated into the Creator's creative imaginative progression of deepening eternal relationships with those who are left to grieve. In our grief, internal and eternal relationships are forged and show those left behind the way to eternity. It is here we become most clear about who we really are.

YOUR TURN

What do you want me to notice today?

_____

_____

_____

_____

_____

How can I get there?

_____

_____

_____

_____

_____

_____

_____

_____

Dying people remind us that…

DAY 25

What do you want me to notice today?

Much of our lives is spent on worrying about the future and reflecting on our past. As a result, we have a difficult time *staying in the moment.* To stay in the present moment requires much concentration. We usually find in rare moments such as these that life has a way of revealing itself to us. We experience surprise as we allow life to unfold in front of us without controlling it with past experiences or future anxieties. It is such a gift to us when these moments inspire us to look into the sacredness of living through the eyes of innocence, purity, and unconditional love.

How can I get there?

To stay in equanimity and not be pulled into our past or our future is present moment awareness. We are free from our experiences on living that tend to cloud our present moment's expressions on living which fill us with spirit. Such inspiration is our natural state of being. There is nothing anyone can do about the past or the future except keep these life experiences from creating present ones filled with their own uniqueness of living not made with human hands, hearts, and minds.

This is all a dying patient has. He or she only has present awareness in front of them. Their next moment could be gone in a single breath. Such sacred moment living infuses these times in our dying days with an eternal awareness. It is an eternal awareness that we could all do well to integrate into our lives long before we die. It is the integrative awareness that life on earth and life beyond time and space seek to find union in a single moment. Such moments of present time awareness is a gift we all have within us. It happens the moment we shift our awareness from human awareness to human sacredness. It is here that heaven and earth meet.

YOUR TURN

What do you want me to notice today?

_____

_____

_____

_____

_____

How can I get there?

_____

_____

_____

_____

_____

_____

_____

_____

Dying people remind us that…

DAY 26

What do you want me to notice today?

Notice what happens when a child is born into this world. They take a deep *breath* in. When we leave this world, we breathe out. It is interesting how this is something that is done over and over with each of us. It is as though we embrace this world in order to live in it. When we take in all the experiences around us and throughout living, it is as though it is digested inside us. We sometimes call this processing the world.

How can I get there?

As you go through the day, notice how you seem to look at the world around you and take it in like we do when we take the next breath. This taking in the world around us appears as though we are breathing it in. Is there a way to take in the world around us without getting attached to what we see and do as though the experiences around us define us?

Dying people are very aware about this type of living as though your next breath could be your last. Each moment is precious to the one reflecting upon the experiences of their lives as though it is in a past that can never be retrieved again physically. This journey into the heart, or dare I say, this journey into the soul of one's existence enables us to find meaning, hope, and unconditional love once known to us at the moment of birth. Such a journey requires us to let go of all the experiences of our past, our present, and our future. As we breathe our last breath out, we become more soul than body until we are fully integrated into who we really are as sons and daughters of the very wisdom that has created us.

YOUR TURN

What do you want me to notice today?

_____

_____

_____

_____

_____

How can I get there?

_____

_____

_____

_____

_____

_____

_____

_____

Dying people remind us that…

DAY 27

What do you want me to notice today?

There are basically two emotions. If you notice, all individual emotions fall into either *fear or love.* Fear fits all the categories of living that effect the ego. Experiences in life that are beyond your control are basically emotionally experienced as being a threat to the ego. Life is not going your way. Love is in the category of unconditional love. Unconditional love experiences deal with how life can shift and change on us at any given moment. This part of us is aware how life is greater than ourselves and how our own individual awareness cannot comprehend why things happen as they do.

How can I get there?

Fear based realities find much of their roots in being in control. Is this a reality? Is this how the world works? It might happen to some degree in one's own little world, but the cost is isolation, loneliness, and emptiness. You are left with the direction of your own little mind, heart, and ego. No one is alone in this world and we have to work with others in order to exist within it. To find real joy, one has to let go of fear and learn to understand and care for others beyond oneself.

Dying patients are on a path that requires and demands them to let go of the ego/self awareness. To be a self aware person is to know where your awareness begins and ends. We do this in order to protect ourselves. There is a greater awareness beyond our own consciousness that brought us into this world and knows how to lead us home. This is the kind of awareness that gives us true freedom. In this kind of awareness, we become connected to the creative force that fashioned and knows every part of us better than we know ourselves. This is the essence of love — to be known as we are known — and to be loved despite ourselves.

YOUR TURN

What do you want me to notice today?

_____

_____

_____

_____

_____

How can I get there?

_____

_____

_____

_____

_____

_____

_____

_____

Dying people remind us that…

DAY 28

What do you want me to notice today?

Strength — Where does my strength come from? I have noticed just how tired I am today. All day, I have been tired. Have you ever wondered what keeps us going at work on those days when we feel like giving up? When a paycheck is involved, we may think of our family. Other times, we may think of being able to spend time with friends. We may think of bills. Hopefully, we think of fulfilling the purpose and the gifts we have to offer others in need of our care.

How can I get there?

As we age, we may find it harder to work in the same way we did when we were in our 20s. We do get physically tired and seem to rely more on the values that motivate us to keep on keeping on. We sometimes go to work with much interest due to doing what we love. We may even love who we work with. But, what if the above is not the case? In this case, we have to dig deep within ourselves for strength that is beyond us. This kind of strength is something you and I are born with the moment we are born. Inside each of us is the ability to make out of any day and any situation a moment of sacredness. If you are lucky enough to enjoy what you do, you are blessed. If you are not doing what you enjoy, you are blessed in the sense of knowing you can make your present situation sacred or find a sacred place to work.

Dying people are not in the best situation for themselves physically. Some look forward to going home and be with those who have died before them. Others may enjoy who they are with and feel deeply sad to be leaving those they love. Others have loved ones in eternity and on earth and feel pulled by both worlds. Whatever the case may be for someone who is dying, one thing is very clear. He or she is on a journey into the unknown. This journey into the unknown has various feelings surrounding what one believes to be their ultimate journey. It is a journey of faith, and one, that has enough strength within it to lead one into eternity itself. Such strength is one that can be trusted. For within such strength we find a place of safety within us that knows we are cared for by the power of a loving Creator. To find this place inside us is to let go of all that we have known and will ever know in the future. Trusting at this level of our being requires letting go of one's physical strength and finding that gentle strength within us called our soul. Here we lay before our Creator every single part of who we are, and trust, that in doing so will emerge the greatest strength on earth and the universe itself.

YOUR TURN

What do you want me to notice today?

_____

_____

_____

_____

_____

How can I get there?

_____

_____

_____

_____

_____

_____

_____

_____

Dying people remind us that…

_____

_____

_____

_____

_____

_____

_____

_____

_____

_____

_____

_____

_____

_____

_____

_____

_____

_____

_____

DAY 29

What do you want me to notice today?

Much of our years in growing up, we tend to think everything in life *matters*. It is as though we tend to think nothing is changing, even though, we and everything is changing all around us at any given moment. The reason is that we tend to think that what matters is matter. Watch what a teenager focuses on. Even before we are a teenager, we need to master this physical body of ours just to live and survive in this world of form.

How can I get there?

A great deal of our attention is on being able to master the world around us, so we can make a good living in the world. Our attention is so great concerning existence that we don't spend enough time in meditation on the things in life that matter the most. As we mature, we tend to focus on the spiritual way of life than we did when we were younger. We may even find ourselves contemplating death a great deal sometime after mid-life. This is when we tend to awaken into soul like no other time in life. We want our life to matter. We want to contribute to the well-being of those we leave behind. We want our life to have meaning and purpose, so we seek for an internal compass to guide us into places only our soul can embrace.

You see, "*the things in life that really matter are the things in life that isn't matter.*" These words came to me years ago, and I am still pondering them from time to time. In fact, it would take an eternity to even get a glimpse of what that phrase really means. Why is it that so much of our existence is spent on finding out what matters, and then, finding our greatest desire the second half of life is finding meaning in what we have been given? Our sacred human quest from here to there and there to here is nothing more than and nothing less that where we place our attention at any given moment. It is as though we begin to see sacredness in every moment. After we come full circle in life, we tend to honor all of life with unconditional love. We end where we begin. This is what matters.

YOUR TURN

What do you want me to notice today?

_____

_____

_____

_____

_____

How can I get there?

_____

_____

_____

_____

_____

_____

_____

_____

Dying people remind us that…

DAY 30

What do you want me to notice today?

You hear a great deal about having a good attitude towards life and all around you. How can this lead to *honoring* what we have been given? Is the key to experiencing goodness through one's attitude? Does it really help? Or, do we find peace through the honoring of what we have been privileged to be a part of through the experiences of our lives?

How can I get there?

Many of us have heard the phrase "fake it until you make it." It is an attempt to alter our thinking on the days we do not feel like showing a good attitude toward life. Our attitude is one way to begin shifting our thinking so our feelings can move to where we can find good in the world around us. In return, we hope to experience this within us. But, do we really have that much control over the world around us?

After working with people who are dying for over 16 years, I have learned that we may not have that much control as we think we may have. When a person is told he/she has months, or even, days to live, it is hard to have a good attitude when their future experiences lead them into such turmoil. What I have noticed is that dying people do find a way to accept or at least acknowledge their future. When the attempts to change the world around us cease and we accept it as it is, something shifts inside us. We move from being in control of our life to getting in touch with a higher power greater than ourselves and seek out to know, to understand, or at least identify with what and whom it is that is governing our universe. This shift in itself allows us to let go of perceived power to find that we are cared for personally and relationally by an authentic power. This view of the world in its purest form and with nothing to hide helps us to realize we are loved with an eternal love and without conditions. We find in such revelations the true meaning of honor.

YOUR TURN

What do you want me to notice today?

_____

_____

_____

_____

How can I get there?

_____

_____

_____

_____

_____

_____

_____

Dying people remind us that…

DAY 31

What do you want me to notice today?

Notice what others *notice.* When you go through your day, notice how much we talk about our experiences. We tend to stay in the intellect much of our lives and throughout our conversations with one another. I want you to pay attention to how much a conversation shifts when one person states that he or she noticed something today.

How can I get there?

Even as you reflect on the image and word "notice" itself, I suspect your attention goes to a place just behind your heart. This area where there is no judgment, no experiences, and nothing to teach someone. It is the area of our lives we experience in soul. We simply state we noticed something to someone and wait for a response. If the person you are relaying this information to does not respond in the intellect and simply notices an experience with you, you will find yourself meeting in soul with another soul.

Dying people do not spend a great deal of their time in the intellect as they get closer to their death. A dying person slows to the point of noticing and slowly experiencing the world around them through their extra sense of perception; rather than, concretely and physically experiencing the world around them. This becoming more soul than body at the end of living enables those caring for a dying person to identify and even connect to the eternal realm of living in a way perhaps never before since their birth. It is though the caregiver is beginning to remember who they are. In a way, it is a remembering oneself into what is most sacred within themselves.

YOUR TURN

What do you want me to notice today?

_____

_____

_____

_____

_____

How can I get there?

_____

_____

_____

_____

_____

_____

_____

_____

Dying people remind us that…

DAY 32

What do you want me to notice today?

What motivates people? Are we a people who move from one desire to the next without direction? Do we live in this world without a purpose and seem to do what we want? After doing this for several years as a young child, we soon find that a life "well lived" is one that is *inspired.* Inspiration is a kind of strength that moves through you and does not come from you. This kind of movement is one that can be focused to do good for others and have tremendous benefits in the lives of others for generations to come.

How can I get there?

Do you remember the last time you went home and you were so tired that you needed to sit because you could not take another step? If you paid close attention, you may have noticed that your attention seemed to move from your head and sink deep into your body. It may have felt as though you were being drained of energy. Out of nowhere your body jerked or moved suddenly. You had energy that you didn't think you had just moments before. It is as though something has just filled your body and mind with energy that is beyond your ability to explain. Inspiration is like that kind of experience. Here, we are filled with energy a cleansing energy enabling us to take the next step in our day.

For years, dying patients and families have inspired me to help them cope in ways he or she may have not thought of on their own. It is true that we need each other to challenge us and motivate us to move and expand our awareness encouraging us to see beyond our own thoughts. Sometimes a dying patient needs this kind of inspiration. We utilize prayer, care, a listening ear, and various other ways to help a dying patient and their families view life beyond what the eyes are seeing in the moment. This kind of care inspires us to look beyond our own needs and wants and view the world around us and within us through the eyes of spirit. Such a journey leads us into a quality of existence whereby what comes through us gives us an inner vision (a filling of energetic spirit in our body) of what life can be.

YOUR TURN

What do you want me to notice today?

_____

_____

_____

_____

_____

How can I get there?

_____

_____

_____

_____

_____

_____

_____

_____

Dying people remind us that…

DAY 33

What do you want me to notice today?

I want you to experience *silence.* Walk through the woods or walk through a garden today. If you will notice, you may feel more relaxed. You may feel more connected to the energy of the sun and plants around you. You may even notice how your thoughts of the day sink into your heart allowing nature's purity to absorb all that is inside you. This movement of your attention into simply becoming aware of your surroundings may even give you a sense of being connected to the earth and all that is around you in a non-judgmental viewpoint.

How can I get there?

Turn you attention toward what lies within you. Your mind will begin to clear. Your heart may become steady. All the thoughts and feelings about your thoughts will begin to fade into becoming aware of your awareness. Once you are distanced from your own personal awareness, you can then be guided into the present moment. Deep within the present moment is a silence - a pregnant silence. It is the place where life is born out of nothingness. This journey into the heart and soul of your existence allows you to let go and relax into who you are.

Dying people are in process of letting go. They let go of the roles he or she played in life as mother, father, brother, sister, friend and more. The deeper a person goes into their silence - the more he or she enters into a spiritual quality of existence. It is our human nature to attach ourselves to people and life in general. It is our spiritual destiny to return to our Creator. This path into "who we really are" is taken in solitude. When we experience silence, true silence of the mind, of the heart, and of the soul, we find "oneness." Oneness is the feeling of being connected to everything and not attached to anything. And, it is found in silence.

YOUR TURN

What do you want me to notice today?

_____

_____

_____

_____

How can I get there?

_____

_____

_____

_____

_____

_____

_____

Dying people remind us that...

DAY 34

What do you want me to notice today?

There are days in our lives when questions on living overwhelm us. As teenagers, we tend to think we have all the answers. The more mature we become there seems to be *more questions than answers.* This shift in our awareness does something to us. We tend to become more tolerant of other points of view than our own. We tend to value relationships outside ourselves as a relief from self-pondering notions that lead our minds and hearts into an endless cycle of self centeredness. The shift of our attention from me to you helps us escape the prison of the intellect and the ego in ways we could not alone.

How can I get there?

Placing our attention on the needs of others is a skill. Just because you can fulfill a need for someone else does not mean you are the person to do so. Others may have better skills to meet someone's needs. This movement from ego thinking that the world revolves around us to the needs of others begin and end there allows an opening. This opening to discern or to go within oneself and evaluate where unlimited resources of living do come from is our connection between heaven and earth.

Dying patients realize in their dying days that life does not begin or end with their birth or their passing. There is the tendency to put life in perspective as we find ourselves letting go of the importance our ego creates. We do need our ego development to achieve experiences in our lives that bring us fulfillment. Our ego knows very little about the world around it. Nor, is it the purpose of our ego as well. When we learn to live with life giving us more questions than answers, we find ourselves returning to the womb of creation. We find ourselves entering into the care and the wisdom that has brought our lives into being.

YOUR TURN

What do you want me to notice today?

_____

_____

_____

_____

_____

How can I get there?

_____

_____

_____

_____

_____

_____

_____

_____

Dying people remind us that…

DAY 35

What do you want me to notice today?

What do you hear in a *story*? Do you just hear the words? Do you simply hear the feelings? Both of these elements are in a story. Do you hear the soul? When a person tells you a story, notice what comes through them. You will find that a story is a person's way of bringing the past into the present. It is a retrieving of one's soul, shared with a friend, and recollected in tranquility.

How can I get there?

In his book "Care of the Soul," Thomas Moore writes that anytime of person utilizes their imagination and heart through the use of story you are in soul. Soul is a quality of existence that is timeless. It is a timeless awareness to the one telling the story. A story told with such vigor that one is led to believe something just happened, even though the story happened long long ago, is a gift. When a person recalls memories that are alive and well within them, they are inviting you to meet them in soul.

Dying patients who come to Hospice Care have a story. He or she may have many stories. Stories reveal a person's character, their wisdom, their love for God, self, and others. A story carries power within it. It is the power to remember an event, person, or place as though the past is relived and just as real in the present. Such a journey into the heart and soul of the one telling a story is a rare glimpse into history. It is somewhat likened to time traveling. When we are transported back in time through the use of someone's need to reveal their soul, we are given an opportunity to evaluate our own stories. In so doing, we may find an inspiration within us that uncovers moments in our own heart and mind enabling our soul to rediscover what has brought us into the world and what will lead us home. It appears magical, and yet, it is who we really are.

YOUR TURN

What do you want me to notice today?

_____

_____

_____

_____

_____

How can I get there?

_____

_____

_____

_____

_____

_____

_____

_____

Dying people remind us that…

_____

_____

_____

_____

_____

_____

_____

_____

_____

_____

_____

_____

_____

_____

_____

_____

_____

_____

_____

_____

_____

_____

DAY 36

What do you want me to notice today?

Today, I want you to notice something about the act of *service*. Service has a way of revealing who we are. In the act of service, the head moves into the heart to be guided by principles and powers greater than our own needs and wants. This journey into the heart and soul of human compassion leads us into the realm of soul.

How can I get there?

Every one of us have something to offer. Each of us have a gift to share. It is only through the act of service to others do we discover and even uncover our greatest capacities and skills that are given to us by God. These gifts belong to no one - not even ourselves. These gifts come through us and not from us. They are gifts of God and from God. When we remember this through service to others, we remember ourselves as we truly are.

Dying patients and loved ones who care for them desperately need the gifts of those who provide an atmosphere for care to come from a place much greater than their personal abilities. Such an atmosphere creates soul care. These skills provide comfort in ways that extend beyond the physical. It is the domain of the Spirit, and as such, allows a dying patient and family to move their attention from the head and into the heart. In this place of awareness, we are each guided into areas of living only our souls can embrace. Healing of the soul illuminates a separation that was never meant to be. Thus, the connectedness we find in sorrow reveals grace occurring in surprising ways. One of which is the pathway into our Creator. Just knowing a person's suffering has an end and eternal peace is around the corner gives even dying patients something to anticipate. It is a lesson the living could do well to learn long before we die.

YOUR TURN

What do you want me to notice today?

_____

_____

_____

_____

_____

How can I get there?

_____

_____

_____

_____

_____

_____

_____

_____

Dying people remind us that…

DAY 37

What do you want me to notice today?

Throughout one's life there will be various forms of *healing*. Healing can come in the form of words, in the form of touch, the presence of a long time friend, and more. Healing implies that a person feels much better than he or she did before the experience of healing occurred. Healing in this sense can mean a relief, a sense of life being brighter, and various other definitions used to describe what happens beyond one' ability to fully comprehend.

How can I get there?

Healing implies openness to living a better life than one perceives it to be in moments of sadness, pain, and grief. Such a journey into the heart and soul of a healing presence requires no effort. It is a person's willingness to belief and trust a pathless path into being created a new being/person. Here we see through the eyes of faith what cannot be seen with physical eyes.

As I serve those who are dying, I will walk into a room filled with many friends and family members. All eyes are on me, I can feel those eyes trying to penetrate my body and wonder who just walked into their space, their environment, or their room. When I introduce myself as a Chaplain, it is known right away that I am there to help. Much of people's attention turn inward into that place we call soul. As everyone's eyes shift from wondering who I am to meeting in a place where introspection and eternal awareness lie, there is a moment of relaxation. Everyone is aware why I am there. This journey into the heart shifts everyone's attention from me being a stranger to meeting in soul. The intensity of uncertainty about who I am and why I am there fades. The need to protect their dying loved one or a patient wondering what is about to happen to them reveals a place where our relationships can be guided by the Creator of us all. Such a sacred space is where God can create a path that leads us all home - in a place we are all known and we are known. The healing of separateness takes shape into a realization we are all children of God, as such, we find our eternal home in and where we presently reside. When the intensity of the eyes fall into a lightness of being, the gentle presence of healing moves our spirit into a healing presence we all can connect with together.

YOUR TURN

What do you want me to notice today?

_____

_____

_____

_____

_____

How can I get there?

_____

_____

_____

_____

_____

_____

_____

_____

Dying people remind us that…

DAY 38

What do you want me to notice today?

I want you to notice the cycle of *birth, living, dying, and death.* There is a pattern to life when you look at awareness and the predictable patterns in nature and in humanity. All life is made up of the same elements. Humanity is aware of our awareness. We have the ability to become conscious of living in a purposeful way like no other creature or entity on earth.

How can I get there?

When a child is born, he or she begins to develop in a way no other person has, is, or ever will on the face of this earth. Each day, a child is learning more about him or herself in ways different than the day before. As a person lives in this life, he or she begins to expand their awareness in ways that allows a certain degree of control in this world. Our ego is developed and we tend to think we are real or vitally important in the grand scheme of things. When a person is told that he or she is going to die, the process of seeing our lives in a less important way integrates itself into becoming <u>a part</u> of the universe over <u>apart</u> from the universe. This movement of returning to the womb of creation from which we came into this world allows a person to become ONE with the innocence we came into the world with in the first place.

Elisabeth Kubler Ross once told a story about two children at a conference I attended. She stated that a child went to a baby crib of it's sibling and asked to be reminded of what heaven is like because he was starting to forget. What if...the purpose of being born into this world is to remember who we really are? What if... we were to remember who we are and live as though we are cared for more than we could really know? What if...a person was to view dying as a movement back into his or her natural state of being? What if...we were to view dying and death as a returning home? "What if"...these two words — are the beginning of what we call an end?

YOUR TURN

What do you want me to notice today?

_____

_____

_____

_____

_____

How can I get there?

_____

_____

_____

_____

_____

_____

_____

_____

Dying people remind us that…

DAY 39

What do you want me to notice today?

Today, I want you to notice *mourning.* Mourning is the effects and affects of the grief process. Basically, mourning is the body's way of expressing itself. Mourning IS the result of loss. When our lives turn to grief over a loss, we feel it in every bone of our bodies. It is a natural way of expressing grief. Our bodies bring forth tears, memories, and emotional expressions allowing those who are in mourning to physically feel the grief over the loss of a loved one.

How can I get there?

Notice how your body is before, during, and after the death of a loved one. You will find that you feel as though something or someone is missing. Your life is not as full as it once was. Your physical life is forever changed and your body will experience this as mourning. Mourning is our body's reflection and expressions of loss. It is a compilation of messages sent to the brain and the heart that something is different or gone. Feeling tired, distracted, without direction or purpose are just a few words and thoughts to remind us we are in mourning.

When a dying person begins to mourn the loss of one's life, there is a unity between the dying body and a person's capacity to identify with a new body. It is a body in transformation. This body appears weaker on one level. At the same time, a body that is in mourning or dying is one that matches what is going on. The body will give cues to the dying person that time on earth as an energetic body is coming to a close, and thus, enables one to start connecting to a spiritual body. A body free from the limits and definitions of our world to comprehend what cannot be understood. This enables a person who is dying or in mourning to identify with what is beyond it.

YOUR TURN

What do you want me to notice today?

_____

_____

_____

_____

_____

How can I get there?

_____

_____

_____

_____

_____

_____

_____

_____

Dying people remind us that…

DAY 40

What do you want me to notice today?

When you see someone cry, experience what is inside those *tears*. Tears are filled with joy and sorrow. They are filled with a lifetime of experiences allowing you and me to experience the fullness of who we are. Tears are reflective. They recall our past and bring them into the present. They are an anointing of the Holy Spirit finding a place in our world.

How can I get there?

Tears are cleansing. They bring a relief or at least an expression to profound experiences being made known to us from the inside out. Tears allow our soul to be made known in our physical world. These tears are more than a memory. They are a living presence within us.

Dying people express themselves through tears. They are nature's way of giving the body a way of releasing much of the stress filling the body with so much pressure. This releasing can be physical, mental, emotional, or spiritual. Usually all of these expressions find themselves in tears. Allow yourself and others to cry. It will lead you to peace.

YOUR TURN

What do you want me to notice today?

_____

_____

_____

_____

_____

How can I get there?

_____

_____

_____

_____

_____

_____

_____

_____

_____

Dying people remind us that...

_____
_____
_____
_____
_____
_____
_____
_____
_____
_____
_____
_____
_____
_____
_____
_____
_____
_____
_____
_____

DAY 41

What do you want me to notice today?

Compassion is when you feel what another feels. You feel another's feelings to the point that the connectedness between you may be closer than it seems. In the health care field, there are times when people in pain reach out in an invisible way for help and support from doctors, nurses, social workers, chaplains and much more. When a person expresses their pain, it has an effect on those around them. Those who can help do and those who cannot physically help look for those who can.

How can I get there?

Have you ever seen a loved one hurt and feel that hurt in the same place? There are some people who are so sensitive that another's pain does become their own. It is important to note that all of us feel another's pain in various ways and depths of our being. We are a people who do want to help.

People who are dying are in a different place the closer to their death they become. They may actually feel for those they are leaving behind a sense of sympathy. Some embrace their dying to the point that he or she is looking forward to the life that is to come. This kind of adventurous spirit allows the dying person to actually feel the fear in those being left behind. A person who is conscious of their living and their dying is aware of awareness to the point of letting go of ego awareness enough to embrace one's most authentic self. This embracing of one's soul to the point of becoming the awareness of peace once sought in living allows a dying person to know they are simply awakening into who they really are. At the moment of death, true compassion is embodied by all when the dying person is free from physical suffering and the loved ones left behind are free from suffering emotionally. Here, one's body has entered into that state of awareness known as "peace beyond all understanding." In faith, the deceased and the loved ones left behind are in the ultimate expression of compassion where souls meet and separation is no longer possible.

YOUR TURN

What do you want me to notice today?

_____

_____

_____

_____

_____

How can I get there?

_____

_____

_____

_____

_____

_____

_____

_____

Dying people remind us that…

DAY 42

What do you want me to notice today?

Have you ever thought of yourself as an angel? Did you know that all the elements that make up all there is "is" in you? Underneath all you see in another person's body such as the molecular structure, dna, atoms, and more lies energy and information. What if you look behind what appears to hide our most authentic self, and find, a part of yourself that is eternal? Did you know that energy and information cannot die? Energy and information can take on various shapes and forms, but it cannot die. We are created for a purpose.

How can I get there?

An angel is known throughout various sacred texts as a "messenger." *An Angel on Earth,* by the above definition could be described as a person. Humans are able to voice what is sacred. Prophetically declare an inner vision as to what is yet to be. We can bring into being what has never been created in the history of humanity with God's help of course. This sacred union between what is eternal and temporal is all contained in the body, and yet, is not fully contained within such an existence for all time to come.

A person who is dying reveals moments of dis-ease in the body. It may be signs of a soul wishing to be set free. When it is time for a soul to return home (heaven), what is created in a person is a disease. Disease takes over the body and destroys the very container holding a soul's release into his or her journey back to our Creator. What we call a death is the destruction of what holds one back from his or her ultimate expression of who we really are - an "Angel of Earth" whose time has come to return to one's most authentic self.

YOUR TURN

What do you want me to notice today?

_____

_____

_____

_____

_____

How can I get there?

_____

_____

_____

_____

_____

_____

_____

_____

Dying people remind us that…

DAY 43

What do you want me to notice today?

Angels of Heaven are those who are more soul than body. Sometimes we experience these entities through happen stance moments when someone appears in our lives for a particular reason(s) to guide us through tough circumstances. Others experience loved ones who have deceased being with them for comfort, grace filled moments, or moments of guidance.

How can I get there?

A heavenly presence will heighten your awareness of the human experience enough to give you faith, hope, and love that is greater than your own power. You will know you are not operating your life experiences on your own. You will know you are surrounded by a great "knowing" you cannot see with your physical eyes alone.

Many dying patients report that they are seeing loved ones who have deceased in their dreams. Some will talk to deceased loved ones in front of you. One thing is very clear, a dying patient is experiencing something that gives them a sense of knowing they are not alone. This assurance is filled with enough love to see them through their dying, and into, eternal life.

YOUR TURN

What do you want me to notice today?

_____

_____

_____

_____

_____

How can I get there?

_____

_____

_____

_____

_____

_____

_____

_____

Dying people remind us that…

DAY 44

What do you want me to notice today?

Have you ever had the experience of someone coming into your life out of nowhere? He or she may have directed or redirected your life from certain doom if he or she had not been there for you at that time. These unexplainable appearances and relationships create miracles. These occurrences give you inspiration and help you connect to what is most sacred to you. It is as though you are destined to be a part of a life path you would not have chosen apart from these relationships leading you to a deeper faith in what cannot be seen.

How can I get there?

I consider *Angels of God* to be experiences leading you into unknown territory and out of the ordinary. For some reason beyond your own comprehension, you trust these relationships as though you have known these angels/people all your life. Their presences may come to you as an inner presence as well, and may even, shift external circumstances to help you fulfill the purpose for which you were born. At times, you may not know why you trust your soul's direction for yourself as though your life depended on it.

Angels of God are not unordinary to the one who is dying. There seems to be an awareness or desire of the heart to look for and even embrace a path into the divine with your whole heart, mind, and soul. I hear people describing to me at times angels that come to them in their dreams or in the night. Some report that they are here to give them direction and things still needed to be done with loved ones who are being left behind in their passing. In any case, Angels of God appear to be more directional and chosen specifically to fulfill God's purpose in a soul's transition from birth to life to death to eternal life.

YOUR TURN

What do you want me to notice today?

_____

_____

_____

_____

How can I get there?

_____

_____

_____

_____

_____

_____

_____

Dying people remind us that…

_____

_____

_____

_____

_____

_____

_____

_____

_____

_____

_____

_____

_____

_____

_____

_____

_____

_____

_____

_____

_____

_____

DAY 45

What do you want me to notice today?

When an infant is brought into the room, a miracle happens. Have you ever noticed how everyone's eyes are captivated by the presence of a small child? They are so tiny, weak, helpless, and in need of an adult's care. Yet, spiritually they have more strength than everyone in that room put together. There is a magnetic power released into a room when a child enters into it. All eyes are upon them and everyone gives them their full attention. The baby doesn't have to do anything - just be there.

How can I get there?

Imagine for a day God's Heart in Yours. Would this change anything? It sure would. People would notice something different about you wouldn't they? They may wonder what has happened and why they are experiencing you in a new way. All of us have a presence about us that others feel. Could you imagine what this would do to your relationships if God's heart was inside yours for a day? It would change things dramatically. I suspect just imagining this experience makes you a little uncomfortable. Yet, God's heart is in you. You are created and fashioned in purity and grace - just like a little baby. You once were that infant. It is still in your awareness. Perhaps, the purity and grace we give a little baby is what we need to give adults in all phases of one's life. It may be the greatest gift of all. To see the innocence of a child inside one another is a great exercise into unconditional grace we all need throughout living.

Dying people return to that place where all of their needs are dependent on others to care for them. To remember we end our lives the way we began it is an interesting concept to ponder. It is to remember we all need one another for love, for care, and for hope. To see into the heart of a dying loved one and find grace and mercy is to find one's soul. It is the place where souls come together and find the little child inside us whose heart embodies the heart of God.

YOUR TURN

What do you want me to notice today?

_____

_____

_____

_____

How can I get there?

_____

_____

_____

_____

_____

_____

_____

Dying people remind us that…

DAY 46

What do you want me to notice today?

Today, I want you to notice *the need for rest*. Grief is hard work on the heart and soul. Loss deepens our awareness of the depths our soul travels in the course of a lifetime. The miles we travel physically is nothing compared to the miles traveled within oneself. We may watch the news and see a tragedy in the making in other countries and our hearts go out to them. The connections made in these moments are far more reaching than miles traveled in our car.

How can I get there?

We need to realize that all of us are connected more than we know, and even, can know. Science tells us that a butterfly that lands on a tree in another country affects us where we are. We are told in grade school that you cannot take a single atom out of the universe without collapsing the whole. This tells me that we are all in this together. To have a heart that cannot forgive or embrace eternity itself breaks our heart into many pieces. It is our ability to know we all need grace and we all need love that enables us to see the world in us; instead of, seeing ourselves in the world. This way, we are all responsible about how we view the world.

A dying patient under Hospice Care enters into a place of silence. It is a place within him or her that is so deep that their loved ones cannot travel with their heart and loss is felt on many levels. This journey into the soul of one's existence and remembering of who he or she is a personal journey between the one dying into eternity and their Creator. And yet, we often deceive ourselves into thinking our loved ones have traveled to a place that is unreachable. When you rest in the knowing that all returns to where we were brought into the world by a power greater than ourselves. We can rest in the assurance of knowing our Creator will give us peace. Just think of this for a moment, your loved one may not have traveled as far as you may think. The moment your loved one took his or her last breath is the same moment they traveled directly into your heart. Listen to your heart, you will find in the midst of your loss the awakening of an eternal relationship with your deceased love one calling you home.

YOUR TURN

What do you want me to notice today?

_____

_____

_____

_____

_____

How can I get there?

_____

_____

_____

_____

_____

_____

_____

_____

Dying people remind us that...

Closing Remarks

"Follow your dreams - Your soul knows the way" by Samuel Lee Oliver. This has been my motto since I have started writing over 2 decades ago. Each article, poem, or book has been guided by the above phrase that came to me years ago. Each of us has a dream just waiting to be born and fulfilled by the dreamer who envisions it. This book is another one of my dreams to find fulfillment in my heart and soul to care for those in need.

This book is transformative. As you have spiritual conversations with your Creator, I hope you realize the various levels of consciousness within you. Each has its own conversation level and ability to reveal to you who you are. I know you will find the greatest journey of living to be the one discovered within you. In the landscape of the soul, the journey of life is eternal and beyond the limits of time and space. Enjoy, it is your soul calling you home from the moment you are born on this earth.

Throughout this book, I have asked you to notice life, spiritual themes, and anything you want to meditate on. Now, I want to ask you to notice the part of you that noticed each moment. Here, you will find your authentic self. It is the part of you not attached to notions moving in and through the world. It is the part of you that is aware of awareness. It is your eternal being. It is where your soul calls home.

I think you will find that you are remembering who you are, more so, than discovering who you are. You are eternal, and the relationships we have with one another will remind you. Your living and your dying are moments of time spent between eternity. As you remember who you really are, you will embrace eternity itself and realize your ultimate experiences are the sacred moments of time where your soul came alive.

The next time you are with someone who dies. I want you to notice something. The instant your loved one breathed their last, and this will always be in the out breath, notice where their soul goes. If you pay close attention, you will notice that their life, their essence, was breathed directly into your heart.

About the Artist

Jeni Huffman discovered a hidden talent emerging from her work with Hospice patients and families. Both, her mom and her dad are artists who met in an art school in Cleveland, Ohio. It appears that their creative talents have been passed along one more generation. From each stroke of her brush, paint, and paper united by an inspired heart, you will experience Jeni's artwork revealing the nature of soul like no other work of its kind.

About the Photographer

Carolyn Dunlavy is a Hospice Volunteer in Northeast Ohio who loves photography. She graciously agreed to photograph the cover of this book with her ability to capture Jeni's artistry with great accuracy and clarity. A big thank you goes to Carolyn's work on this project.

About the Author

Sam has cared for the needs of the dying in palliative care for over 16 years. During that time, Sam has served as the Chair, and now, Co-Chair of the Hospice Ethics Committee at the Hospice Care Center of VNS in Akron, Ohio. He has served several years as a State Continuing Education Chairperson for the Association of Professional Chaplains. For well over a decade, Sam has been an active editorial review board member and contributing writer for Healing Ministry Journal, The Journal of Terminal Oncology, and The American Journal of Hospice and Palliative Care.

Sam began his speaking about spiritual care over 15 years ago and continues to speak at public engagements on the local, national, and international levels. He has spoke at several college campuses and keynoted at several Hospice Conferences. His first book of six *"What the Dying Teach Us: Lessons on Living"* is a National Hospice and Palliative Care Organization selection.

Sam's undergraduate study was at Georgetown College with a B.A. in Psychology. He received his Master of Divinity @ The Southern Baptist Theological Seminary in Louisville, Kentucky with an emphasis in the Pastor/Teacher track. In 2003, Sam Oliver finished his post-graduate certificate in Health Care Ethics through Rush University in Chicago, IL. Presently, Reverend Doctor Samuel Lee Oliver is the Chaplain at the Hospice Care Center in Ohio.

To order more copies of this book, please contact

Fideli Publishing

www.fidelipublishing.com/bookstore

or call toll free

888-343-3542